SIDEBOARD IN THE QUEEN ANNE STYLE.

100 Victorian Architectural Designs

for Houses and Other Buildings

A. J. Bicknell & Co.

Dover Publications, Inc.
Mineola, New York

Bibliographical Note

This Dover edition, first published in 2002, is an unabridged republication of the illustrations and text from the work originally published in 1878 by A. J. Bicknell & Co., New York, under the title *Specimen Book of One Hundred Architectural Designs.*

Library of Congress Cataloging-in-Publication Data

Specimen book of one hundred architectural designs.
　　100 Victorian architectural designs for houses and other buildings / A.J. Bicknell & Co.
　　　　p. cm.
　　Originally published: Specimen book of one hundred architectural designs. New York : A.J. Bicknell & Co., 1878.
　　ISBN 0-486-42155-4 (pbk.)
　　1. Architecture, Victorian—United States—Designs and plans. 2. Architecture, Domestic—United States—Designs and plans. 3. Architecture—United States—19th century—Designs and plans. I. Title: One hundred Victorian architectural designs for houses and other buildings. II. William T. Comstock Company. Specimen book of one hundred architectural designs.

NA7207 .S69 2002
724'.5—dc21

2002018921

Manufactured in the United States of America
Dover Publications, Inc., 31 East 2nd Street, Mineola, N.Y. 11501

Fig. 1.—Front Elevation.

Low priced Cottage. From "Bicknell's Village Builder and Supplement." One large quarto vol., 77 plates. Price $10.00.

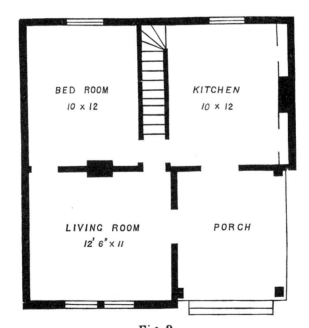

Fig. 2.

First Floor Plan.

Cheap Country Cottages.

THE designs on pages 5, 7 and 8 represent three cheap but at the same time tasty and convenient country cottages, for men of moderate means. These designs are shown on plate 1, Bicknell's "Village Builder and Supplement." The estimates, in work named, of the cost of these buildings, are : for Fig. 1, $750; while if the design of Fig. 3 be used,

Fig. 4.

$1,000, and for Fig. 5, $1,200. These prices, however, do not include the cost of cellars, although in many localities they could now be executed, including cellars and everything complete, for prices named. The scale of the drawings is $\frac{1}{8}$ in. to the foot. Fig. 2 is the ground plan, and requires no particular explanation. The second floor plan would contain the same number of rooms, and of the same size given on Fig. 2, except as they would be reduced by the necessary closets. The run of the stairs to be toward the centre of the house, and the stairs to be lighted from the roof. Figs. 1 and 3 give elevations, in different styles, of this design ; and Fig. 4 shows a section of the wall corresponding to Fig. 1. We give a general specification and bill of materials, with ample allowance for necessary waste, adapted to New York ideas, based upon Fig. 1, leaving prices to be carried out according to cost in different localities. The outside sills to be 3x6 inches, with cross-sill 6x8 inches under partition between living-room and bed-room. Flooring joists 2x8 inches, 16 inches on centres, running from front to rear. The outer ends in the second floor to be set upon 1x4 inch pieces let into the wall studding (2x4 inches), and the inner ends to be carried by the partition. Steep rafters, 2x5 inches. Upper rafters, 2x6 inches. The estimate includes the cost of a cellar 7 feet deep under the whole house.

BILL OF MATERIALS.

Excavation, 28 cords.

800 cubic feet stone wall, @ — cents.

4500 bricks for chimneys (one 8x12 flue to each) and underpinning wall (2 feet high and 8 inches thick), @ $— per m. laid.

3000 feet b. m. framing stuff, including partition studs, @ $— per m.

1200 feet wall lining (1 inch thick), planed and matched, @ $—.

7 windows complete (including plain beaded casings), @ $—.

2 outside doors, complete, $—

12 inside doors (including hangings and casings) @ $—

1500 feet b. m. roofing boards, those on porch roof and projecting eaves, as well as the rafters over the same, to be planed, @ $— per m.

6½ squares slating, @ $— per square.

6 squares tinning, @ $— per square.

1500 feet b. m. flooring boards, 1¼ inch thick, planed and matched, @ $— per m.

45 yards lathing, with one coat plastering, for ceiling of cellar, @ — cents per yard.

325 yards lathing, with two coats of plastering, @ — cents per yard.

Porch, eaves, corners, water-table, etc.

800 feet b. m. interior finishing stock, for base, stairs, shelves, etc., @ $— per m.

Extra hardware and metal.

Carpenter's work, besides that included in above items,

Painting,

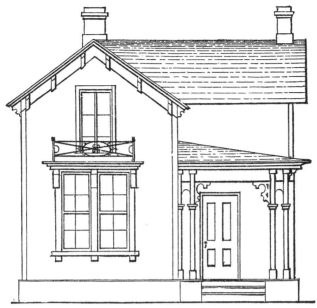

Fig. 3.—Front Elevation.

Fig. 5 (page 8) gives the elevation and Fig. 6 the ground plan of a second design, much more complete than the one shown and described on preceding pages.

The stairs to the second story (design, page 8) should be finished with newel-rail and balusters of some hard wood. The passage to the cellar to be inclosed by a partition beneath the outer string of the stairs. The qualifications of the previous estimate will, of course, apply to this design.

BILL OF MATERIALS.

Excavation, 38 cords ....

7100 bricks, @ $— per m.... ....

920 cubic feet stone wall, @ — cents........

4200 feet b. m. framing, @ $—..............

2500 feet b. m. wall-lining, @ $—... ....

1400 feet roofing, @ $—..................

2000 feet b. m. flooring, @ $—........ .....

1200 feet b. m. interior finish, @ $—..... ..

Carpenter's work in above items...........

10 windows and 14 doors (complete).........

Stairs.....................................

140 lineal feet eave-cornice, with tin gutter..

70 lineal feet rain-water leaders, @ — cents.

Porch, water-table, etc.....................

13 squares slating, @ $—..... ....

1½ squares tin (on porch roof), @ $—.......

78 yards one coat plastering (with lathing), @ — cents...............................

480 yards two-coat plastering, @ — cents. ..

Painting................. ....

$

The second story contains three bed-rooms and two closets, which are shown to working scale in Bicknell's "Village Builder and Supplement." One large quarto vol., 77 9 x 12 plates. Price $10.00.

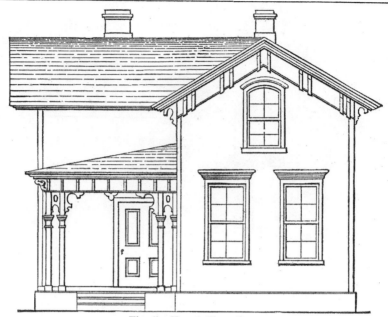

Fig. 5.—Front Elevation.

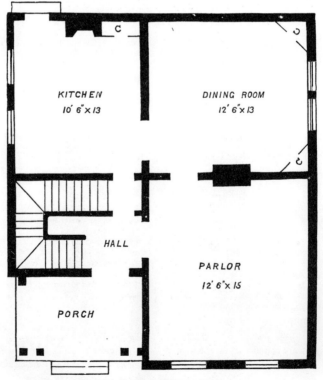

Fig. 6.—First Floor Plan.

City Residence. From Cummings' "Architectural Details." One large quarto volume 56 plates. Price $6.00.

Reduced Elevation of Suburban House, design 1, "Supplement to Bicknell's Village Builder." Large quarto volume, 20 plates. Price $4.00.

An Ornamental Cottage Design,

COSTING FROM $2,000 TO $2,500.

THE illustrations on following page show the right elevation and first-floor plan of a very pretty Swiss Gothic
Cottage, from Atwood's " Modern American Homesteads," which
contains three additional elevations, four plans, and principal
exterior and interior details—46 plates in all.   Price $2.50.   The
same is also published to working scale, including specifications,
price $10.00.   The first story is very commodiously arranged.
The broad piazza runs nearly the whole length of one side, as
shown on plan.   In the second story are four good-sized bed-
rooms, arranged around a central hall, besides a press or store
closet, which might be turned into a commodious bath-room.
The attic consists of a single large bedroom, having windows
on all sides.   The exterior of the building is very tastefully
ornamented in rustic style with wood-work trimmings, the
whole presenting a very handsome and artistic appearance.

Right Elevation.

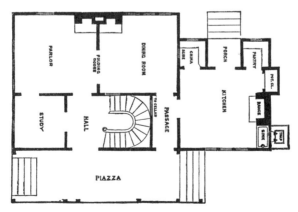

First Floor Plan.

VIEW BEFORE ALTERATION.

We offer the cuts represented on this and the following pages as an example of remodeling. The cut on this page is an exceedingly plain yet substantial structure, such as may be found in any New England village. That on page 13 represents the same building modernized sufficiently to meet the requirements of present tastes, and is a good example of re-

VIEW AFTER ALTERATION.

modeling at small expense. On the right of the house is a piazza connecting with the adjacent room by French Windows opening to the floor.

For further examples of remodeling, both exterior and interior, we refer to the work from which this house is taken— Woollett's "Old Homes Made New." A neat little oblong volume of 22 plates, just published. Price $1.50.

A PICTURESQUE COUNTRY VILLA.

It is quite possible that propositions which are mathematically accurate may not be true in practice. Thus while it is true geometrically that a circle encloses the greatest amount of space with the least length of boundary, it is not true architecturally. Led astray by the obvious correctness of the mere geometrical part of the proposition, certain reformers at one time carried the principle to an extreme, and we had a very loud and persistent advocacy, not only of square houses, but of those of which the ground plan was in the form of an octagon, the nearest practical approach to the circle. But practically it was found that mere quantity of cubic contents is not the only thing that is required. Availability is quite as important as quantity, and hence it is found that convenience and utility, as well as appearance, are promoted by a departure from the bare rectangular form. The accompanying design illustrates this point very well. By abandoning the old "dry goods box" style, the arrangement of the rooms and their individual comfort and convenience is greatly increased, while to the appearance of the whole there is given such character and picturesqueness as will add greatly to the value and attractiveness of the property. A special and somewhat new feature is the location of a conservatory in front of first landing of stairway in octagon end at the right and dressing-room below. The library is in the rear of main hall, and at the right of back hall, which includes the back stairway. The parlor occupies the front of the house at left of hall, with dining-room, butler's pantry, store room, china closet and dumb waiter in the rear. The plan is arranged for kitchen in the basement, although it can easily be included on principal floor if desired. The second floor contains three bedrooms, bath-room, and five closets. Two or three rooms may also be included in the attic plan. The estimated cost in vicinity of New York is $4,000, although in many sections it may be executed at a cost of $3,000 to $3,500.

The elevations, plans and details are shown on plates 45 and 46, "Bicknell's Cottage and Villa Architecture." One large quarto volume, 66 plates. Price $6.00.

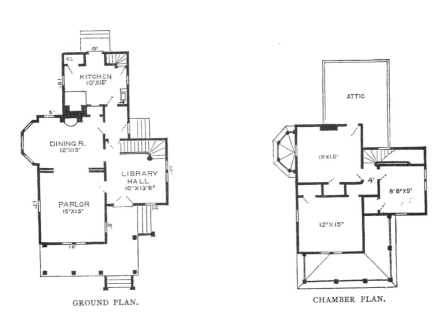

GROUND PLAN.   CHAMBER PLAN.

From Hussey's "Home Building." One quarto volume of 42 plates, showing 45 original designs of medium and low-priced buildings. Price $5.00.

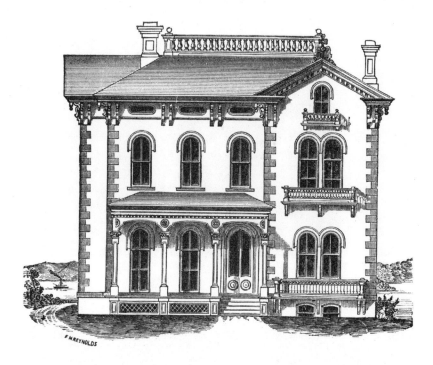

DESIGN OF A SUBURBAN RESIDENCE.

We present herewith a design of a suburban residence, to be built of brick with stone trimmings. It should occupy a somewhat spacious lot, and be so situated as to give the dining and sitting rooms a cheerful and sunny aspect, and secure the front entrance against the penetrating blasts of winter. The principal hall is spacious, having no stairway to obstruct it. The interior finish should be in keeping with the general design; the roof can be of tin or slate, the latter being, of course, far preferable and the cheapest in the end.

This house was erected some time since at a cost of $10,000, but with the present low prices of materials and labor could now be built at from thirty to forty per cent. less.

Full plans and elevations of this design, drawn to an eighth-inch scale, are given in the "Village Builder and Supplement," a work containing 77 plates of practical designs, sent free of charge to any address on receipt of ten dollars.

Plans suitable to this elevation will be found on plates 7 and 8, " Supplement to Bicknell's Village Builder," a large quarto volume of 20 plates. Price, $4.00.

FRENCH COTTAGE.

We give above a front view of a French Cottage of moderate accommodation. The lower floor is devoted to the parlor, dining-room and kitchen; the parlor has a bay window, facing the street; the bay window on the right opens from the dining-room; the kitchen is immediately back of the hall, and has an entry to the rear and a door entering the dining-room. Two windows light the kitchen—one on the left, not shown in this view, and the one to the left of this view, looking toward the street. On the upper floor there are three chambers and one bed-room, well supplied with closets. This design can be executed at an expense of from $2,000 to $3,000, according to locality and style of finish.

The plans and elevation of this cottage are represented on an eighth-inch scale in the Supplement to "Village Builder," a work containing 18 practical designs, mainly in the French style. Sent post-paid to any address on receipt of $4.00.

A MODERN VILLA RESIDENCE.

Mr. Woollett, in his book on "Villas and Cottages, or Homes for All," describes a villa of frame structure designed for erection on a stone foundation, with cellar, with heavy sill, corner posts, girts, and plates, and filled in with brick. The house being intended for a central location between other buildings on a lot of moderate width, has a nearly symmetrical front. Individuality is given to the details by using panels and bands covered with cut shingles, instead of clapboards on rough boarding. The roof is also covered with shingles, and both those of the roof and band are painted in deeper tints than the main wood-work.

The finish of the interior is to be in white ash and butternut. There are four good-sized rooms and pantry on the first floor, the parlor and dining-room being at the left and the sitting-room and kitchen at the right side of the house. All these rooms are well lighted, airy, and cheerful. The second story contains four bed chambers, bath-room, and three large-sized closets.

The estimated cost of this house was $8,000, in 1876, but at the present reduced prices of labor and material, could now be built for about $6,000.

This cut is reduced from design 4, Woollett's "Villas and Cottages," where are also given the first and second story plans, drawn to scale. One oblong volume of 40 plates, giving plans and elevations of ten villas and ten cottages. Price, post-paid, $3.00.

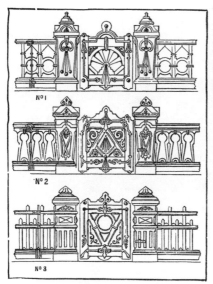

Miniature cut of plate 7.
Published size inside of margin, 9 x 12 in.

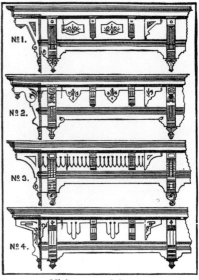

Miniature cut of plate 12.
Published size inside of margin, 9 x 12 in.

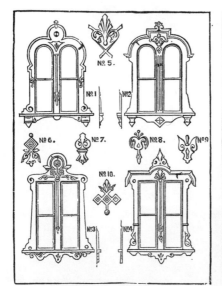

Miniature cut of plate 43.
Published size inside margin, 9 x 12 in.

Miniature cut of plate 49.
Published size inside margin, 9 x 12 in.

Scale indicated on plates.

From Croff's new work, mainly on Details, entitled "Progressive American Architecture."
One large quarto volume, 97 plates. Price, $6.00.

Perspective view and first floor plan of design shown on plates 3 and 4, "Bicknell's Village Builder and Supplement," which contains elevations, plans, full specifications and form of contract. One large quarto volume, 77 plates. Price, $10.00.

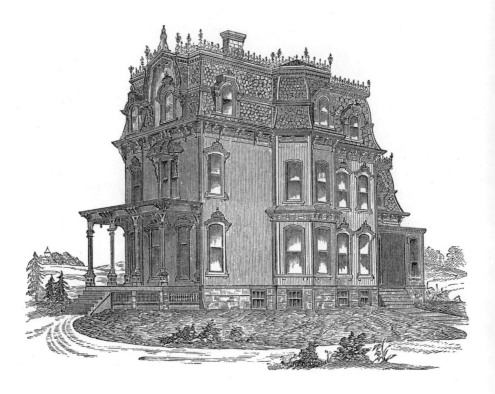

The above cut represents a very elegant suburban house, double French or concave and convex roof. This design is the first of its class erected in the vicinity of New York, but since its completion this style has become quite popular and been followed in several instances. This house, known as the "Case House," is situated in the City of Elizabeth, New Jersey, and is regarded one of the handsomest in the city.

This selection is taken from Bicknell's "Detail Cottage and Constructive Architecture," one large quarto volume of 76 plates, price, $10.00, where are also given front and side elevations, details, and first and second floor plans, drawn to working scale.

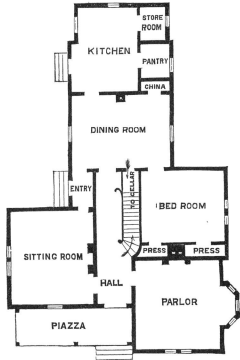

Perspective view and first floor plan of design shown on plate 13, Supplement to "Bicknell's Village Builder." One large quarto volume, 20 plates. Price, $4.00.

FARM HOUSES.

From Allen's "Rural Architecture." A complete description of farm houses, cottages and out-buildings, comprising barns, wood-houses, tool-houses, carriage and wagon houses, ice-houses, apiary, poultry-houses, piggery, etc., etc. Fully illustrated. Price $1.50.

VIEW OF HALLWAY.

We offer this cut as an example of remodeling. In the original house the stairway was narrow and enclosed. This has been removed, and a new staircase in hard wood introduced, with fire-place and settle at the foot of the same, and at the end of the settle the old hall-clock. The upper portion of this fire-place has the brick-work exposed, the lower portion being encased for mirror, &c., and above the mirror a small sconce mirror. As will be noticed, the doorways into the principal rooms from this hall are without doors; a curtain of heavy material, hung to a rod with rings, forms a means of shutting off the view from the Hall when desirable. The end of the main hallway is marked and divided from the staircase by a Newell column bracketed each way.

The above selection is from Woollett's "Old Homes Made New." One oblong vol., 22 plates. Price, post-paid, $1.50.

Fig. 3, plate 55, "Cummings' Details."   One large quarto vol.   Price $6.00.

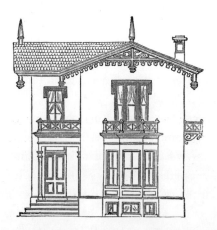

Reduced elevation of Fig. 1, plate 5, Bicknell's "Village Builder and Supplement."
One large quarto volume, 77 plates.   Price $10.00.

A Screen of Books. From "The House Beautiful." By Clarence Cook. One 8vo
volume, beautifully printed and very fully illustrated. Price $7.50.

Design for Mantel, from page 175, Gardner's "Home Interiors." One 12mo volume,
cloth, containing over 60 illustrations. Price $1.50.

The above superb mantel is made of richly carved marble, but a more simple one may be substituted ; and we offer it, more to show a tasteful and artistic arrangement, than for the mere form of mantel.   An improving effect is produced by applying heads found on *cretonne* or in the Decalcomanie designs, or more artistic still by using photographs, to silk merino or any smooth cloth, arranging one as a medallion in the center of each lambrequin point, then surrounding with embroidery.   The antique fire screen in front of the grate may be beautifully imitated by a painting in Grecian style, or it may be embroidered in silk or Berlin wool-work at pleasure.

The above cut and description are taken from " Beautiful Homes, or Hints in House Furnishing," by H. J. Williams and Mrs. S. C. Jones.   A beautifully illustrated volume of 314 pages, cloth.   Price $1.50.

DESIGN FOR A PARSONAGE HOUSE.

The parsonage house, of which a perspective view is given on this page, was built in Matteawan, N. Y.   Local stone was used in its construction, the quoins and belt courses being of a good quality of brick.   It contains, on the ground floor, a parlor, study, chamber, dining-room, butler's pantry, and kitchen, with side and back entrances.   Present cost, $8,coo to $10,000. The effect of the whole building is unique in the extreme, and its commodiousness and convenience must at once be recognized.

This view is taken from Bicknell's "Detail Cottage and Constructive Architecture," where are shown perspective view, front and side elevation, and two floor plans.   Price $10.00.

Illustration from "Beautifying Country Homes." A hand-book of Landscape Gardening, by J. Weidenmann. Containing 17 full-page and 7 double-page colored lithographs of places already improved. Price, prepaid, $15.00.

View of picturesque villa, shown on plate 20, Croff's "Progressive American Architecture.'
One large 4to volume, 97 plates.   Price $6.00.

View of Residence, of which elevation and plan are given on plates 36 and 37 of Croft's
"Progressive American Architecture."   One large 4to volume,
97 plates.   Price $6.00.

Summer House. Shown on plate 21, Bicknell's "Detail Cottage and Constructive Architecture." Large quarto vol., 76 plates. Price $10.00.

Stairway shown in Loth's "Practical Stair Builder." Large 4to vol., 30 plates. Price $10.

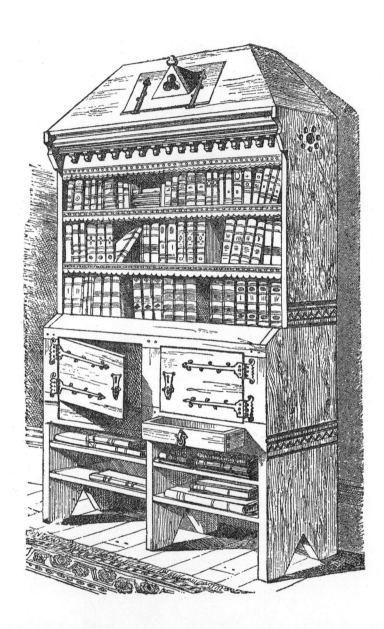

The above cut represents a " Book-Case," executed from a design by Chas. L. East-lake, and is here given as an illustration from " Hints on Household Taste," a work of 304 pages 8vo, very fully illustrated ; price $3.50.

Frontispiece of POTTERY AND PORCELAIN. By WILLIAM C. PRIME. Illustrated. 8vo, Ornamental Cover, Gilt Tops and uncut edges, $7 00.

Reduced Elevation of design plate 11, "Supplement to Bicknell's Village Builder," which shows eighteen working plans.   One large quarto vol., 20 plates.   Price $4.00.

View of Court House, suited to plans shown on plates 49 and 50, Bicknell's "Village Builder and Supplement."   One large quarto vol., 77 plates.   Price $10.00.

ON A SIDE HILL.

This cut represents quite a picturesque little story-and-a-half Cottage, and is selected from Gardner's "Homes and How to Make Them,"—a very desirable little book, containing letters between an American Architect and his friends, giving hints and suggestions relating to the building of homes. Illustrated by several views. 314 pages, 12mo. Price $1.50.

The above cut represents a very commodious English Cottage, and is known as the "Judge's House" in "Illustrated Homes," where will be found floor plans of first and second story, and description, in form of conversation between the architect and his client. This cottage can now be executed for about $3,000. This book contains 287 pages. 12mo. Price $1.50.

City Store Front.

WE give on the following page an elevation for a city store front; it is arranged with an important and conspicuous flight of stone stairs to the upper stories. This gives picturesqueness to the façades and increases the importance of the whole upper part of the building. This is one of the constructive features which, instead of being ignored or hidden away, is made to play a prominent part in the architectural treatment. It is the same with the girder over the broad store front; this is made to look like iron, since no other material used in a horizontal mass will satisfy the necessity of supporting the brick-work above. This girder, with its broad bearings on the substantial bracketed piers, gives a gratifying sense of security. These features, although purely constructive, can be made as rich with appropriate decoration as the mass of meaningless features so often seen.

The almost invariable absence of any apparent means of support for these broad arches so frequently-occurring in store fronts of late, leaves an unpleasant feeling of insecurity, although we know that in most, if not in all of these cases, the arch has ample invisible means of support in the way of iron ties, or arched iron girders concealed by the masonry.

In these days of so much sham building, straightforward dealing with honest construction will give the beholder at once a comfortable sense of substantial security, and help to raise architecture to its proper position in the arts.

This design is taken from the work entitled "Bicknell's Street, Store and Bank Fronts," containing 22 plates, showing 34 designs of Street Fronts for Dwellings, Stores and Banks, including several plates of details. Drawings to scale. Price $4.00.

Elevation of a City Store Front.

FIRST BAPTIST CHURCH,

ELIZABETH, N. J.

Country Church.　Design from "House of God."　One Small volume, containing views, plans and sections of several Churches; price, post-paid, $1.75.

Design for a Chapel Church.

SEE FOLLOWING PAGE.

THE Illustration shows the front elevation of a church edifice, with accommodations for about seven hundred persons. It is intended to be built of stone or brick, with cut-stone dressings, although the same design might be carried out in wood. The entrances are numerous and conveniently arranged, as well as amply large. In the front is a vestibule, 9 feet wide, extending entirely across the building, containing four entrances to the audience room, as well as the stairs to the small gallery above. The audience room is 60 x 70 feet, with a chancel 20 feet wide at the end opposite the principal entrance, containing the pulpit or any other arrangements which denominational peculiarities might require. There are 136 pews on the principal floor, with five sittings in each. The organ is on one side of the chancel, and on the opposite side is a minister's retiring room. Access to the audience room is also had through vestibules on either side, and these vestibules communicate with the vestry and committee rooms. The vestry is 40 x 48 feet, the committee rooms each 18 x 20 feet, communicating with each other by folding or sliding doors, and also with the vestry by means of sliding sashes in addition to the ordinary doors. Above the committee rooms, and reached by an ample flight of stairs from the vestibule below, is an additional room for the use of the ladies of the society. All these various rooms should be abundantly lighted and well ventilated. The expense of the building would of necessity vary much with different localities, and with the amount of cut stone used upon the exterior; but under favorable circumstances it might be built of stone for about $20,000.

Elevation of Chapel Church.   Reduced from plate 42, Bicknell's "Village Builder and Supplement," in which the plan is shown and description given.   One large volume, 77 plates.   Price $10.00.

SOUTH NYACK CHAPEL.

A WAYSIDE SABBATH-SCHOOL CHAPEL.

Situated on the river-side road, a mile below Nyack, on the Hudson, is a chapel, 24 x 40 feet, built of brown stone, quarried from the neighboring hills. The interior is finished in walnut and chestnut oiled ; the cross-beams 'or rafters are finished in their natural wood, and are appropriately lettered in Scripture mottoes ; the walls are kalsomined a neutral tint, and a suitable border runs round the ceiling and wainscoting. The building will seat two hundred comfortably. The seats in the nave of the chapel have alternately reversible backs, and those on the sides are half-circles for Sabbath-school classes. On the walls are appropriate engraved pictures ; and altogether it has a cosy, attractive look, inviting to all who enter.

This design is given in elevation and detail in Atwood's "Modern American Home-steads." 8vo, cloth. Price $2.50.

FIRST PRESBYTERIAN CHURCH,

OF HIGHLAND FALLS, N. Y.

SEATING CAPACITY, - - - 264.

From "Withers' Church Architecture." One large volume of fifty-one 9 x 14 plates, substantially bound in extra cloth; sent by express to any part of the United States, upon receipt of price, $15.00.

View of Chapel with Bell Gable.   From Withers' "Church Architecture."   One large
volume of 51 plates.   Price $15.00.

Opera House and Library. From Bicknell's "Public Buildings." Containing 21 plates of Elevations, Plans and Details. Price $3.50.

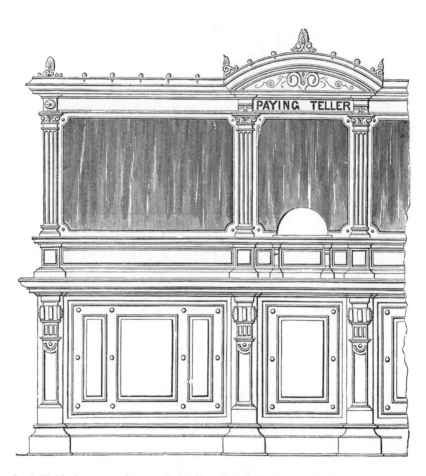

Bank Finish shown on plate 60, Bicknell's "Detail Cottage and Constructive Architecture."   One large quarto volume, 76 plates.   Price $10.00.

Bank Front. From "Croff's Progressive American Architecture." One large quarto
volume, 97 plates. Price $6.00.

VEYSEY HOMESTEAD COTTAGE.

The "Veysey Cottage" was erected recently in the picturesque village of Tenafly, N. J. Present cost about $2,000. This
sum includes a large school-room communicating with the
dining-room, and a cellar and finished attic of four rooms. The
interior finish corresponds with the ornate style of the exterior.
The materials were selected and first-class of their several kinds,
and constant supervision given to the execution of all the work.

From Plate 1, Atwood's "Modern American Homesteads."   One 8vo volume, 46 plates
Price $2.50.

Design for a Cottage, by E. C. Hussey, Architect.

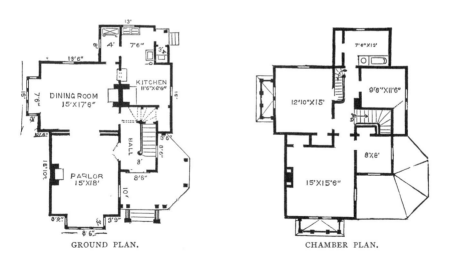

GROUND PLAN.   CHAMBER PLAN.

From Hussey's "Home Building." One quarto volume of 42 plates, showing 45 original designs. Price $5.00.

The above cut shows in miniature a few of the designs and details in "Bicknell's Detail Cottage and Constructive Architecture," containing 76 9 x 12 well filled plates, all finely lithographed, including 8 plates in color.   Price, post-paid to any address, $10.00.

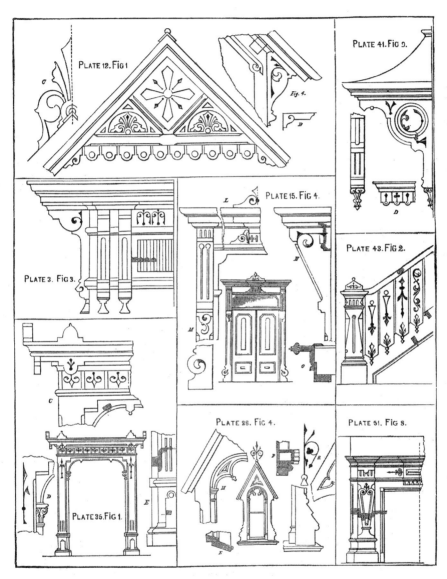

Designs (reduced from plates indicated) from Cummings' New Book, entitled "Architectural Details," containing 387 designs and 967 illustrations of the various parts needed in the construction of buildings, public and private, both for the city and country ; also plans and elevations of houses, stores, cottages, and other buildings. One large quarto volume, 56 plates. Price $6.00.

Design for a Country House.

THE dwelling shown on the following page was erected at different periods; the main building in 1868, and the later additions, consisting of laundry, dining-room and dinner-service rooms and pantries, in 1870, making a 16-roomed villa of superior accommodation. In remodelling, many difficulties were surmounted of an architectural and constructive kind to obtain that complete unity of style apparent now. This is emphatically a modern homestead, as every appliance for making the house service systematic, safe and pleasant was employed here. The materials of construction were wood, the frame sheathed and felted, the roof slated, and the interior finish tasteful and sufficiently elaborate to harmonize in character with the style of the house. A stable called a "cottage stable" was enlarged at the same time, and a gas-house built, with fixtures for lighting the dwelling. The cost of the first contract was $8,000; of the second, $6,000; and of the third, $4,000. The same could now probably be executed complete at a cost not to exceed $8,000 to $10,000.

This design is from Atwood's "Modern American Homesteads." One 8vo vol., 46 plates. Price $2.50.

Design for a Country House.

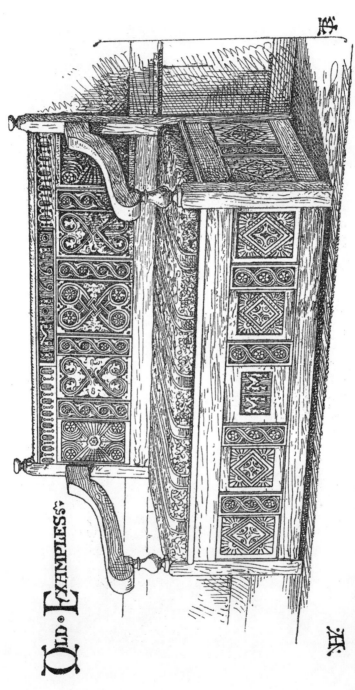

Example of Ancient Furniture, from a new publication, entitled "Examples of Ancient and Modern Furniture, Metal-Work, Tapestries, and Decorations," by B. F. Talbert, Architect. This book, which is very finely printed, contains many exceedingly interesting drawings, most all in antique style, which may furnish useful hints to such architects and manufacturers of furniture who aim at the production of something different from the prevalent and too common style. This illustration, which is taken from this work, represents a settee of a genuine ancient design, a style which at the present day has been introduced with great success and general approval in a very large number of the most fashionable residences in New York City. One folio volume, 21 plates. Price $8.00

PERSPECTIVE VIEW.

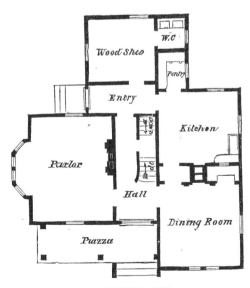

FIRST FLOOR PLAN.

From "Supplement to Bicknell's Village Builder," which shows Plans, Elevation and Details. One large quarto volume, 20 plates. Price $4.00.

View of School-House, representing Eveleth's "School-House Architecture."   One
quarto volume.   Price $4.00.

View of Stable, representing Harney's "Barns, Out-Buildings and Fences."   One quarto
volume, nearly 200 designs.   Price $4.00.

View of Country House, representing Vols. I. and II., Woodward's "National Architect." Quarto volumes of 100 plates each. Price per vol., $7.50.

A Suburban Residence. From Woodward's "Suburban and Country Houses." One small volume, containing 20 designs. Price $1.00.

Design from Hussey's "Cottage Architecture."   One quarto volume.   Price $4.00

Reduced cut of Perspective View, plate 28, Woollett's "Villas and Cottages."   One
volume oblong 8vo, of 40 8 x 12 plates.   Cloth.   Price, post-paid, $3.00.

Miniature cut of Front Elevation, design 3 plate 4.

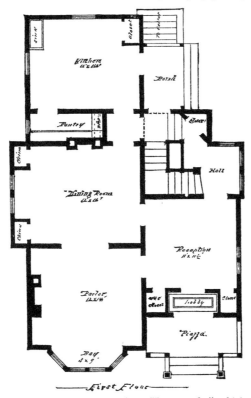

Taken from Atwood's "Modern American Homesteads," which shows three plans and three elevations of this design, drawn to scale. One 8vo volume, cloth, 46 plates. Price, post-paid, $2.50. This cottage can now be executed at a cost of $2,200 to $2,800 according to locality and style of finish.

Reduced cut of Elevation, plate 50, "Detail Cottage and Constructive Architecture."
One large quarto volume, 76 plates.   Price $10.00.

Tower Cottage.   From "Detail Cottage and Constructive Architecture."   One large
quarto volume, 76 plates.   Price $10.00.

AN ORNAMENTAL COTTAGE.

The accompanying view, designed for a gardener's cottage, shows a building, small, but very picturesque in appearance. It would be very suitable for a gate-lodge, or a seaside or summer cottage, and would look extremely well among the trees of a camp ground. The living room is of good size, well lighted by a square bay window. The kitchen is well supplied with closets. The second floor contains three bedrooms, very conveniently arranged, and each provided with a closet. The two downstairs rooms and the large front bedroom are supplied with open fireplaces, the value of which for ventilation is so often overlooked in cheap houses; besides this, there should be ventilating tubes or shafts in the chimney side, with registers opening from each room, thus insuring a good system of ventilation. The roof should be ventilated by openings under the projecting eaves. The estimated cost of this building is from $1,200 to $1,500, according to locality and style of finish.

We make this selection from Bicknell's "Cottage and Villa Architecture," one large quarto volume, 66 plates, including specifications for frame and brick dwellings, price $6.00, where may be found the plans of this design drawn to scale.

French-Roofed House, with Tower. From Reed's "House Plans for Everybody." A new work, fully illustrated with many designs and plans, some of very low cost, to which are added careful estimates of materials, labor, etc. Price $1.50.

Half Timbered Cottage. From Atwood's "Country and Suburban Houses." Illustrated with about 150 engravings. Price $1.50.

QUEEN ANNE MANTEL, WITH MIRROR.

FROM WARREN WARD & CO.

Fig. 3.

Fig. 2.

Fig. 1.

Fig. 1.—SIDEBOARD. This illustration is taken from a Black-Walnut Sideboard of the Queen Anne period. It is relieved by English tiles above the shelf, and is a very handsome piece of furniture.

Fig. 2.—MANTEL. This engraving is from an Ash Mantel, plain, massive and rich.

Fig. 3.—NEWEL. Black-Walnut Newel Post, very unique and handsome.

ALL FROM WARREN WARD & CO.

PARLOR SUITE.

FROM WARREN WARD & CO.

This is engraved from a suite in the Queen Anne style, covered with raw silk. The suite is composed of seven pieces, and is very stylish and at moderate price.

CHAMBER SUITE No. 1.—From Warren Ward & Co.

This suite, made after Eastlake's designs, either in Ash or Black-Walnut, is very chaste and elegant, and is finished with either marble or wood tops. The pieces are: a Bedstead, French Dressing Bureau (French Plate Glass, 30 x 20), Washstand, Table, two Chairs, Rocker and Towel-Stand.

CHAMBER SUITE No. 2.—From Warren Ward & Co.

This is a very stylish suite, after English designs, made both in Ash and Black-Walnut, and composed of the same pieces as No. 1. This is made with the Dressing-Case as illustrated and with the French Bureau.

H. W. JOHNS'
ASBESTOS
LIQUID PAINTS.

These Paints are in every respect strictly first-class, and are warranted unequalled by any others in the market in purity, richness and permanency of color, beauty of finish and durability. They are prepared ready for the brush in sixteen newest shades and standard colors, suitable for the tasteful decoration of all classes of buildings, inside and out, and for all purposes where a perfect protective coating is required. Owing to the wonderful *covering* properties of these Paints (two coats of which are fully equal to three of any other), the farmer, merchant or manufacturer can, by their use, preserve and beautify their buildings, fences or other wood and iron work, at from one-half to two-thirds of the usual cost of other ready-mixed paints, or white lead and linseed oil. They contain no water, alkali or other useless or deleterious adulterations or dilutions, such as are used in nearly all the liquid or so-called chemical paints, and are *guaranteed* to be *the most durable paints in the world for exposed wood and iron work.*

☞ *The contract for supplying paints for the Gilbert Elevated Railroad of New York City was awarded to us. This is the largest contract ever made for painting any single structure in this country.* ☜

Roof Paint—for tin and shingle roofs, iron work, agricultural implements, fences, out-buildings, etc. We guarantee this to be a better and more economical paint than has ever before been offered to the public for similar purposes.

☞ *This Paint was used with entire success, when all others failed, upon the roof of the Exhibition Buildings at Philadelphia, the largest area of tin roofing in the world.* ☜

Fire-Proof Paint—for the protection of inside wood-work of factories, bridges, boiler-rooms, and other wooden structures in danger of ignition from sparks, cinders or flames.

☞ *This Paint has been applied to more than 4½ acres of wood-work in the two immense dry-goods stores of Messrs. A. T. Stewart & Co., of New York City* ☜

ASBESTOS ROOFING,

with WHITE FIRE-PROOF COATING. This well-known Roofing is now in use in all parts of the world, and is the only reliable substitute for tin. It is adapted for steep or flat roofs, and forms the handsomest, coolest, and most durable portable roofing made. In rolls ready for use. Easily applied by any one. Costs only half as much as tin.

☞ *This roofing is used in preference to all others by the Kingsford Oswego Starch Factory, Remington & Sons, and by the most extensive Manufacturers, Builders, Railroad Companies, etc., in the United States.* ☜

Asbestos Steam Pipe and Boiler Coverings—consisting of *Asbestos Cement Felting and Air Chamber Coverings.* Prepared ready for use. Easily applied by any one. The most durable, effective and economical appliances known for preventing radiation of heat ; will save from 25 to 40 per cent. of fuel.

☞ *Used by the United States Navy Department and in the most extensive public buildings.*

Asbestos Boards for Gaskets, Steam Packing, Sheathings, Fire, Acid and Water-Proof Coatings, Cements for Gas Retorts, Leaky Roofs, etc.

☞ All these materials are prepared ready for use, and can be easily applied by any one. ☜

LIBERAL INDUCEMENTS TO GENERAL MERCHANTS & BUILDERS.

Send for Samples, Illustrated Catalogue and Reduced Price-List, etc.

H. W. Johns Mfg. Co., 87 Maiden Lane, New York.

GARNKIRK CHIMNEY TOPS.

After many years' use in this country, the Chimney Tops of the GARNKIRK FIRE CLAY COMPANY have been found to resist the action of coal gas, and of wet and freezing weather. They all tend to improve the draft : and those marked as Windguards are especially useful where, with the wind in a certain direction, there is a tendency to occasional puffs down the chimney.

Their use makes the chimney a pleasing feature of a dwelling, and in many cases, at a cost no greater than that of common brick-work.

To give the best effect, the brick-work should be built up a short distance above the roof. The tops may be set on the bricks in cement or mortar, but it is better to let them into a stone cap made to cover the brick-work and project over it.   Pattern Sheets will be sent on application.

E. D. BASSFORD,

COOPER INSTITUTE,

House-Furnishing Hardware,

China, Glass, Cutlery and Silverware.

Houses,

Hotels,

Steamships,

Yachts,

Schools,

AND

Public

Institutions,

COMPLETELY FITTED OUT.

Dinner, Tea, Toilet and Table Wares,

From the plainest for every-day use to the richest and most elaborately
decorated ; also

CUTLERY AND SILVERWARE, COAL VASES AND HODS, FIRE SCREENS,

COOKING UTENSILS,

AND ALL KINDS OF TIN, IRON, COPPER, BRASS AND ENAMELED
WARES, WOODENWARE AND REFRIGERATORS,

AT GREATLY REDUCED PRICES,

40 to 60 Per Cent. below Usual Retail Rates.

EDWARD D. BASSFORD,

COOPER INSTITUTE,

Corner Third and Fourth Avenues and Eighth Street, New York City.

GOODS PROMPTLY DELIVERED.

50-page Price List and Refrigerator Lists mailed free on application.

NEW YORK

SAND BLAST WORKS,

145 & 147 Mulberry Street,

One Block East of Broadway, near Grand,

Ornamental Glass & Glassware.

SARGENT & BURGER, Proprietors.

———o———

Estimates promptly furnished.   Price List
sent on application.

———o———

Ornamental Glass,

FOR PUBLIC BUILDINGS AND PRIVATE
RESIDENCES,

SAND BLAST, CUT AND EMBOSSED.

———o———

**Table Ware Engraved in the Best
Manner.**

———o———

GROUND GLASS A SPECIALTY.

———o———

ZINC GRAINED AND PREPARED FOR
LITHOGRAPHIC USE.

Being the sole proprietors of the

SAND BLAST,

we are prepared to do all ornamental glass work for Buildings, Banks, Offices, &c., as well
as *Colored Signs and Globe Work,* at the most reasonable rates.

Giving our individual and personal attention to the work, we are enabled to execute
all orders for *Etched or Sand Blast Work* with promptness and care.

We will furnish *Architects, Builders, and all who contemplate Building
or Remodeling* with pattern sheets or designs on application, with estimates.

NEW YORK SAND BLAST WORKS, 145 & 147 Mulberry St.

METALLIC SHINGLES.

PATENTED SEPT. 4, 1877.

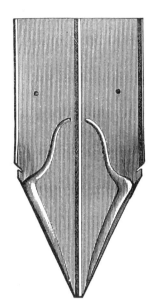 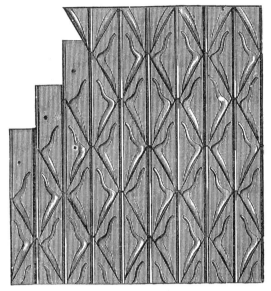

MAKE THE

Cheapest Fire-Proof Roofing.

Highly ornamental. Can be laid by any carpenter. About one-fourth the weight of slate. Cannot be broken by frost or otherwise. Not affected by expansion or contraction. Requires no repairs. Easily transported. Samples at our New York Office, 23 Cliff Street, and A. J. Bicknell & Co.'s Office, 27 Warren Street.

SEND FOR FULL DESCRIPTION AND PRICE-LIST TO THE

IRON CLAD M'F'G CO.,

50 GREENPOINT AVENUE,

P. O. Box 2528, New York City.   **BROOKLYN, E. D.**

THE YALE LOCK

MANUFACTURING CO.,

OFFICE AND WORKS, STAMFORD, CONN.

SALESROOM, 53 CHAMBERS ST., NEW YORK.

ARCHITECTS not provided with our large illustrated catalogue are requested to so notify us, and it will be forwarded to them without charge.

We respectfully invite attention to our several lines of Locks and Real Bronze Hardware. We make no *second grade* work, "brass plated," or otherwise. Our goods will always be found to be exactly what they appear to be, and we mean them to be always *the best* in their respective classes.

THE YALE LOCKS.

A complete line, including Rim and Mortise Door Locks, in great variety and an assortment of Cabinet Locks for drawers, desks, chests, etc. These locks are especially for use where *security* and *non-interchangeability* of keys is an object.

THE "STANDARD" LOCKS.

A complete line of mortise locks, applicable to all the various sizes and kinds of swinging and sliding doors. The design and workmanship of these locks are of the best.

THE YALE BRONZE GOODS.

A full line of Knobs, Butts, Bell-pulls, Bolts, Hinges, Sash and Shutter Trimmings, etc., etc. All of these goods are of the best quality of *real bronze*.

The Burglar-Proof Sash-Lock, illustrated above, indicates the general character of these goods.

Beware of Deceptive Imitations not bearing our Trade Mark.

ARCHER & PANCOAST M'F'G CO.,

DESIGNERS AND MANUFACTURERS OF

FINE GAS FIXTURES,

Artistic Bronzes, Antique Candlesticks.

Mantel and Table Ornaments, Sconces, &c.

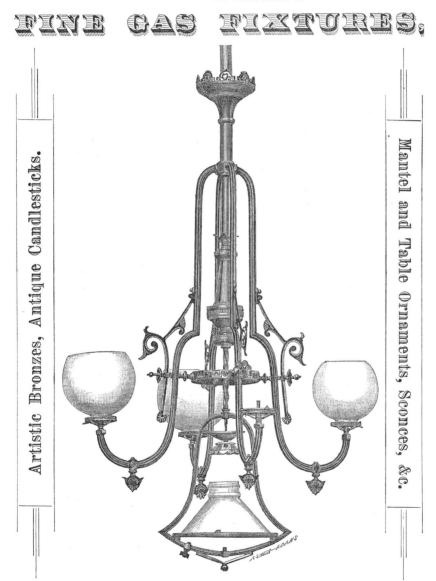

CHURCH METAL FURNITURE.

67 GREENE STREET,
68, 70 & 72 WOOSTER STREET, } ABOVE BROOME. { Broadway and University Place
Cars pass our Showrooms.

NEW YORK.

ESTIMATES SENT ON APPLICATION.

MINTON'S TILES,

ENCAUSTIC AND PLAIN

FOR FLOORS,

AS LAID BY US IN THE

CAPITOL AT WASHINGTON,

*And in numerous Churches, Banks, Court-Houses, County Clerks' Offices,
and other Public Buildings, and in the best Dwellings
in every part of the Country.*

THEY ARE USED FOR

Vestibules, Entrance Halls, Hearths, Conservatories, Etc.

ALSO

Hand-Painted Art Tiles, Glazed, Enamelled and Majolica Tiles, in rich Colors,

For Mantels, Fire-Places, Hearths, Door-Frames, Wainscoting, &c.

BOTH KINDS ARE USED IN

BANDS & PANELS FOR EXTERIOR DECORATION,

ALL AS EXHIBITED AT PHILADELPHIA.

Pattern Sheets and Prices will be sent on application ; and when required,
careful workmen will be sent to lay floors.

PORTLAND, ROSENDALE & OTHER CEMENTS,

FOR SALE BY

MILLER & COATES,

279 PEARL STREET, - - NEW YORK.

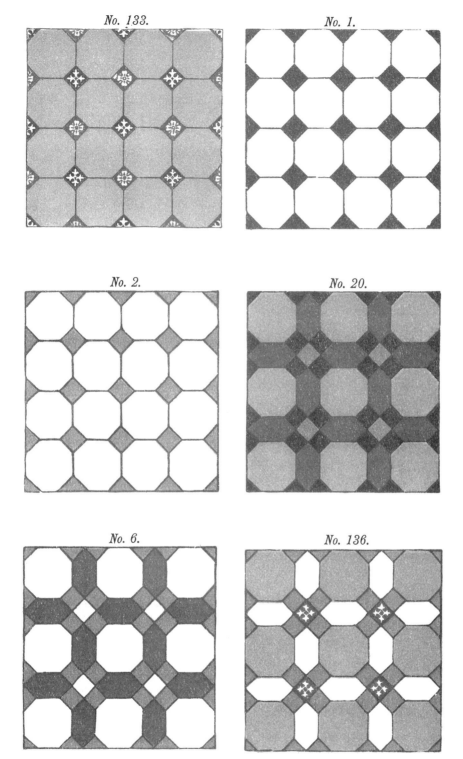

No. 133. No. 1.

No. 2. No. 20.

No. 6. No. 136.

Patterns of Minton's Tiles for Floors,

FOR SALE BY

MILLER & COATES, 279 PEARL ST., NEW YORK.

Other Patterns with prices will be sent on application.